" To Adell "
To God Be The Glory "
Happy Birthday !
—Sweether Jim 2

Sweether Simmons

Down, But Not Out!

Reflections of a Hurricane Katrina Survivor

by
Sukether Williams Simmons

Bloomington, IN Milton Keynes, UK

authorHOUSE™

AuthorHouse™
1663 Liberty Drive, Suite 200
Bloomington, IN 47403
www.authorhouse.com
Phone: 1-800-839-8640

AuthorHouse™ UK Ltd.
500 Avebury Boulevard
Central Milton Keynes, MK9 2BE
www.authorhouse.co.uk
Phone: 08001974150

First published by AuthorHouse 4/25/2007

ISBN: 1-4259-4284-9 (sc)

*Printed in the United States of America
Bloomington, Indiana*

This book is printed on acid-free paper.

ACKNOWLEDGEMENTS

First, let me start by saying 'TO GOD BE THE GLORY FOR THE THINGS HE HAS DONE FOR ME! I thank him for allowing my family and me to survive the floodwaters of Hurricane Katrina. I also thank God for allowing me to see through the darkness into his marvelous light, which revealed my life's purpose. Because of him and only him I live to tell the story of his grace and mercy so others may know the truth.

Second, I would like to thank my husband and friend Cedric Simmons for his strength and encouragement needed to remain focused on my dream. I would also like to thank him for bringing me back to the place where I belong; I love you!

To my son Cedric Jr., thank you for your praises, and great ideas on marketing. To you I give simple motherly advice, always put God first, remember to give him the praise and all your ideas and plans will become a reality, continue to follow your dreams letting no one stop you (smile) also continue to believe in yourself, make it happen, I know you can, Love You!

To my baby Alex (A J.), thank you for allowing me to share Roger's story with the world and thanks for always bringing a smile to my face every single day! Also thanks for writing that sensational poem "WANTED" now the whole world can see how wonderfully talented you are!

To my sisters, Glenda, Nancy, Sadie, Kirsten, my mother-in-law Jean, and my sister in-law Melissa (Missy) thanks for allowing me to share our story " Sleeping With The Enemy" with the world even though it was a difficult time we managed to get pass all the craziness and see the humor, I think all of you are special ladies, Love ya!

To my niece Kori, thanks for all your help with the computer I could never have done it without you! Keion, thanks for your help with power point! Hey Kira, thanks for showing me a quick and easy way of doing things. God has blessed each of you with bright talented minds he expects you to continue to use them! (Look out world here they come!).

To my brother Riley just wanted to say Hi!, To my sister and friend Pat, thanks for everything (the list is too long to name) you have been a blessing in my life, who would believe the two of us could be so much alike it's sometimes scary, same birthday, same likes and dislikes I truly think we are sisters in real life! To my girls Donna, and Lois we will be friends till the end, love ya girlfriends! To Steph, Flora, Jane, and Paula the Original girlfriends! I can't forget to include my big sis. Glenda, To Mr. Wilbert Jordan thanks for your subtle criticism and legal advice (even though I sometimes accepted it kicking and screaming!) and thanks for helping me to realize my potential. To Morris Dillard, thanks for always willing to help me out, you are a jewel, don't ever change! To all the wonderful people in Lake Charles Louisiana and in San Antonio Texas, to all the Volunteers around the country, thanks for everything, the work you do and have done for me and all the Hurricane Katrina and Rita survivors really means a lot ;I know I will never forget it! Thank you Anderson Cooper for reporting our stories to the world with compassion, standing with us through it all and never letting our stories die, also a great big Thank You to CNN! And special thanks to Tom Joyner and The Morning Crew for always being there for the People, and to OPRAH, you are an angel on earth, thank you from the bottom of my heart! And to the many people around the world who generously donated time, money, support it will always be remembered, THANKS.

TABLE OF CONTENTS

BRIDGE OVER TROUBLED WATERS

SUKETHER'S LAGNIAPPE

DOWN, BUT NOT OUT!
Reflection of a Hurricane

Katrina survivor

THE WAY I SEE IT

We can write about our struggles
We can write about our pain
We can write about our victories
And demand change
In order to embrace our future, we
must understand our past
To learn what it really means to be free at last

Hurricane Katrina brought tears to our eyes, but
Out of the floodwaters our people will rise
Many souls perished, but the strong survived
Through their pain, and suffering this country will heal
Sighting social and racial injustice as real

The eyes of our savoir are never asleep
He sees all evil and deceit
To kill our spirit it takes more than a hurricane,
What will it take to make America feel shame?
You see it as a disaster; I see it as a victory
The world got a chance to see America's hypocrisy

The picture in my mind
Is very clear
Hurricane Katrina revealed the truth
That's the way I see it
What about you?

DOWN, BUT NOT OUT!

They say New Orleans has seen its last days
To make a come back there is no way
Throw in the towel and give up the fight
We had our chance to get it right
Our politicians trade deals for a name
Louisiana politics will never change

Everyone is handing us the towel
We're going to win this fight somehow
Because a fighter is down on the mat
Doesn't mean he can't come back
All polls have us down for the count
We may be down, but we're not out!

We evacuated from the storm
The levees gave way, now our homes are gone
When the time is right, we're coming home
We've already been away too long

They say hurricane season is only months away
Debris from Katrina is still in the way
Money from the government is coming in slow
Corps. of Engineers is asking for more
It looks like it's over without a doubt
Because we're down, doesn't mean we're out!

They say the city will never be the same
Sell your homes before the next hurricane
You have your opinions and we have our beliefs
It's hard to understand what you can't see

(Cont.)

They say we can't win with a losing hand
Our beaches and coasts are waste land
We're not giving up without a fight
This is our land and we have rights
All polls have us down for the count
We may be down, but we're not out!

MY SOUL LOOKS BACK AND WONDERS
The Recap

Today I am a displaced person by no fault of my own. Every morning I awake 'MY SOUL LOOKS BACK AND WONDERS' how this came to be. I went from a hard working, tax paying, law-abiding citizen, with a sometimes-dysfunctional family, and an aspiring writing career to a displaced Hurricane Katrina survivor. The events that led to my unfortunate demise are somewhat overwhelming.

IN August of 2005, a hurricane entered the gulf, and with each day it intensified, it increased danger to the city of New Orleans. The hurricanes' name was Katrina. One day she was heading for the Florida Keys; the next day she would be heading in the direction of New Orleans. For days Hurricane Katrina toyed with the city like other hurricanes in the past causing much uncertainty. While most citizens evacuated before the predicated landfall others procrastinated.

Everyone hated routine evacuations including myself. They were stressful and costly. Most of the time they consisted of enough food and water for two days per person, a two-day change of clothing per person, and a two night's minimal stay in a shelter or hotel. Extra cash on hand was always necessary for evacuations and sometimes the lack of made evacuating difficult. I like many New Orleanians made a decision to evacuate the day before all hell would break loose. However, a few people did ride it out; consequently, they would suffer hurricane Katrina's wrath first hand.

Louisiana is known for its unscrupulous political wheeling and dealings. History is riddled with facts and fictional accounts of underhanded, under the table, and backroom deals. The City of New Orleans is certainly no exception. The wheeling and dealings in the past has always raised eyebrows but never before has it affected as many lives as the Levee Board's decision to gamble on Levee restoration.

Today my home, job, cars, and cherished possessions are gone. My family and friends are scattered across the country. I am dishearten and in total disarray regarding what has happened.

Hurricane Katrina made landfall on August 29, 2005 my oldest son's birthday. Katrina dealt the city a huge blow. She blew in packing one hundred and thirty mile per hour winds; violently uprooting trees, demolishing homes and businesses; sparing nothing. She will enter the history books as the deadliest hurricane in US history, and I along with the entire nation bared witness.

News stations around the country reported New Orleans as surviving by a narrow escape, before actually assessing the damage. Then unexpectedly water began seeping into the streets. In a matter of minutes, it was pouring in at full blast, and a calamity of events would soon unfold.

New Orleans Levee Board officials have known for a long time the levees were in poor shape. Their concerns were, if a hurricane above a category three should ascend upon the city, levees would fail. They feared storm surges producing levee breaches could flood New Orleans washing it off the maps; However, each year the matter of repairs was discussed and set aside (nothing was done). The Board's decision to gamble with our lives has cost us just that, one roll of the dice and it is gone.

Hurricane Katrina's strong force winds wrestled with New Orleans levees causing them to fail as predicted, consequently floodwaters spilled over into the streets, and canals producing a deadly aftermath.

The images coming out of New Orleans horrified us all. City Officials were unaware of the abundance of people left behind. There were old people, young people, men, women, and children in floodwaters pleading for help. Many clung

7

to floating objects such as tables and crates. Those with boats used them to patrol the streets rescuing people from the violent waters. There were also hundreds of people trapped in their homes and stranded on rooftops. A large number of abandoned animals also needed rescuing.

Everyone was in search of shelter, because of the City's mandatory evacuation order, there was none. The New Orleans Super Dome opened at the last minute, only to the elderly, and those with special needs. Because it was the only shelter, it filled quickly.

The unexpected flooding along with its victims unfortunately caught everyone off guard. Therefore, it was not enough food and supplies to go around, and not enough security.

Those stranded were mostly the poor and African Americans with no financial means, or transportation. They came from every direction unfortunately there was no place to go. The Ernest M. Morial Convention Center was forced to open as a temporary holding area for victims until help arrived. At the site, survivors were met with more disappointments. There was no food, water, medical assistance or information and in anguish, survivors waited.

On a bridge, leading to the superdome helpless others gathered. Because there was no room inside the dome, or center they camped in the hot sun, wet, hungry, and despaired. The media reported their stories as the world watched in disbelief. Everyone wanted answers. Where was the emergency response team, and when was it coming?

Officials and citizens alike became very irate with the Federal Government's slow response to this critical situation. Four days passed before the government would take action.

Every aspect of the city was in complete chaos. Reporters looking to make a name for themselves capitalized on the situation by distorting their reports. Some reported stories of widespread looting by New Orleans Police officers and citizens. Others reported unconfirmed stories of suicides, rapes, and murders committed inside the superdome and convention center. Reports of gang violence and hostile take over spread throughout the city. The exposed bodies of the dead and faces of helpless Americans appeared before the world.

The authorities themselves spun out of control as many of their own officers abandoned ship. The city switched to automatic pilot leaving everyone feeling uneasy in the city known as the "BIG EASY". City officials and the media seriously stressed the need for urgent assistance. The National Guards soon arrived to help restore law and order. Every newsstand and television station reported the City's demise. The city that care forgot quickly became the city our nation forgot.

In the days that followed, confusion and lack of communication aroused between government, state, and local officials. As conditions, worsened anger and frustration mounted; then the finger pointing began. The government's slow response for aide added explosives to an already erupting volcano. The dismal images projected across televisions throughout the country became impossible to overlook. Underprivileged Americans depicted as "refugees" raised questions regarding Americas' definition of equality.

Who was responsible for this depiction of a Third World Country, (isn't this America?) Why did we not aide our own? Who is at fault the Federal Government, state or local officials, or is it the people themselves? Was the government's inaction a result of issues involving race or class, or both? The government's inaction received strong reaction from around the world; every world leader was demanding answers.

Sadly, Louisiana is a state divided by much more than Parishes and its most popular city New Orleans became a perfect example. Before the hurricane, New Orleans came alive with music and culture. Its Cajun cuisines have delighted many a palate. African Americans were the majority but had very little authority. There were the upper to middle class whites, the upper to middle class African Americans, and New Orleans poor who lived in neighborhoods rarely seen by tourist.

The poor lived in the poorest sections of the city, and in some of the city's housing developments. Most worked, but still earned wages at or below the poverty level. Like most New Orleans communities, these areas are close knit because of their culture, but here the bond between family and friends is so strong it sometimes protects those who break the law. There are many who want to get away from the shootings, gang violence, and drug crimes but have little or no financial means. Others have accepted the violence as a way of life. City government practically abandons and ignores their plight, causing the racial and economic divides to become clearly visible. On August 29, 2005, the world got a look at New Orleans forsaken people.

The cameras caught on tape a side of New Orleans the world would have probably never gotten a chance to see. What they saw beyond Bourbon Street, the French Quarters, and the beautiful Garden District is a city divided by racial, social and economic inequality. The cameras caught New Orleans on tape, but who is filming most of the major cities across America?

Hurricane Katrina did not discriminate. Ironically, for a short time Katrina became New Orleans great equalizer. For the first time white, black, rich, and poor could be seen standing in lines across America seeking assistance for the same basic needs.

Katrina no doubt was a massive destroyer of lives; however, it inadvertently helped to restore lives. The hurricane forced many of New Orleans poor into cities that offered better living situations; causing those who were receptive to restore their confidence, and hopes for a better way of life.

Today I am a hurricane Katrina Survivor. I to like so many have suffered a lost; but in the process, I have gained much more. We have all paid a high price for a very important lesson. My life is a perfect example how material things hold little value when you can walk away from a catastrophic Hurricane like Katrina. Katrina has also given me a chance to reflect and make changes in my life that not only benefits me but others as well.

Now, as I find the strength to pick up the pieces of my life "My SOUL LOOKS BACK AND WONDERS" was Katrina a good thing or bad thing, was the damage done by hurricane Katrina; or was it already there? Will we learn our lesson, or will history repeat itself? There are a lot of areas we will need to look at in the future, but right now the city is very much in need. I pray my city, the New Orleans I know and love, will one day return to a viable, flourishing city once again. I hope we can learn from our past mistakes as painful as it is. It will take all of us to turn things around. We need everyone regardless of race or class to be part of the rebuilding process. It will be up to the citizens to decide if we will return to the old ways, or adopt a new and better way of life for all. We have a lot of work to do in a city where people proudly proclaim 'New Orleans, Love It or Leave It!'

WHY DIDN'T SOME LEAVE

If you haven't walked a day in their shoes
It's easy to decide which one to choose
Why didn't some leave the world wants to know
Without hearing their stories, we will never know

Some trusted their faith against the hurricane
Strong sentiments caused others to decide in pain
No money, no credit, no transportation for some
With no available means, where can one run?
Not all decisions make perfect sense
Sometimes it's a matter of dollars and cents

Many too weak to travel stayed behind
Others too stubborn rode it out one more time
Some gambled Katrina would go the other way
While others didn't have anything to say

The people, its officials, they all had a choice
Much could have been achieved if they spoke in one voice
The world got a look at New Orleans dark side
An ugly picture to the world they couldn't hide
Not all decisions make perfect sense
Sometimes it's a matter of dollars and cents

AMERICA'S CRIME

Hurricane Katrina came ashore stripping
New Orleans to its very core,
Innocent people were caught in her
path leaving a deadly aftermath.
Uprooted trees, houses off slabs, windows
blown out, the city trashed
Storm surges, levees breached, floodwaters
covered houses and streets.

The city's poor left behind, a society created by design.
Voices could be heard crying in the
dark as families were torn apart;
Massive destruction of enormous size claimed
men, women, and children's lives.
.Invisible people the poor became as help
from officials reluctantly came.
The world watched in total disgrace as
officials apologize for the delay.
For days, the city became unmasked sighting
discrimination of race and class.
The media covered their sorrowful stories as
love ones around the world worried.

America is always the first to give aide,
but to its own help was delayed.
The President says, "I accept full blame" as
FEMA, declares there will be a change.
To New Orleans poor we apologize, for
turning a deaf ear and closing our eyes.
The effects of Katrina will be felt for a
time so will America's ugly crime.

A BUREAUCRATIC CRIME

My home is in ruins
By no fault of mine
Worked all my life, did what's right
To become government victimized

They predicted this would happen
A long time ago
They knew the levees would fail
And Mr.Go should go (Mississippi River Gulf Outlet)

Now the damage is done
And everyone's pointing blame
We all have become victims
In this bureaucratic game

In all my years of living
I've never seen anything like this
There are no clear choices
There is no easy fix

Someone should be held accountable
For decisions proved unwise
No amount of money
Can replace human lives

The government says it's sorry
As if they really care
But we're the one's left
With this heavy cross to bare

(Cont.)

Senate committees meet
But no one will admit
Bureaucratic red tape
Is nothing but bull----

Now the damage is done
And everyone's pointing blame
We all have become victims
In this bureaucratic game

ANGELS IN OUR MIDST

The day before Hurricane Katrina hit New Orleans my family and I along with extended family members totaling twelve in all evacuated with only the necessary essentials such as food, water and two days of changing clothes. With our destination uncertain we followed the contra flow of cars heading west in search of higher ground and out of the destructive path of the hurricane. Traffic moved slowly as people anxiously made their way west, because of the large number of last minute evacuee's traffic was almost at a stand still. We fled the city like the Children of Israel trying to escape Pharaoh's wrath, but instead of Pharaoh, our tormentor was Hurricane Katrina.

We arrived in Lake Charles Louisiana hours later; a drive, which normally takes four hours by car suddenly, took eight hours. Exhausted from lack of sleep and the long ride, we exited off Interstate 10 in search of a hotel or an evacuation shelter. We found a shelter a few blocks from the interstate down from a gas station. We really didn't want to go into a shelter; but with limited funds between us we didn't have much of a choice. Reluctantly we headed to the shelter to bunker down for the night, but before checking in we stopped by the nearest gas station to fill up. I happened to notice a hotel to the right of the station, after passing numerous hotels along the way, all of them displaying a" NO VACANCY "sign I almost hesitated to stop. I checked the hotel out, and to my surprise, there was one vacancy left. It was a room with two doubled beds. I had found a needle in a haystack, but there were twelve of us. Everyone was given a choice; we could ride the hurricane out together in the hotel room or anyone who wanted to could check into the shelter down the street. Everyone chose the cramped quarters of the hotel room.

We settled in for a long night anxiously awaiting the arrival of Hurricane Katrina, and anticipating an end to this dreadful ordeal. We watched the news hanging on the reporter's every word, praying for Katrina to make a turn, but our prayers went unanswered. Early Monday morning just after daybreak, Hurricane Katrina made landfall in New Orleans as a category three; news stations around the world reported the event.

The hurricane breached levees destroying the city, producing flooding up to ten feet or more in some areas. There was no turning back for us now. With limited funds, we planned our next move. The hotel manager could no longer accommodate us another night. The stress and stain of our entire situation left us frustrated, as we tried to find a place to go. Check out time was at eleven o'clock and time was running out. I approached the front desk once again in hopes of a miracle, and surprisingly that's exactly what I got. The manager informed me that we could have the room for one more night. This was both a blessing and a relief.

The next day we had to move on, but it wasn't going to be easy. Everyone had good ideas and suggestions, but no one had money. With the clock winding down, I decided to consult with the man upstairs. Upon my return, I had received three phone calls; the first was from a friend of ours who wanted to help financially. The second was a message from the hotel manager informing us that we could stay another night, and the third call was from our family in San Antonio Texas with news of an available house, which could accommodate all twelve of us. My prayers had been answered!

Thank God for the kindness of strangers. The same day we received the phone calls we met some wonderful people like Teddy, Francis, and Milton who lived in the area. After hearing our story, they invited us to their home for a wonderful feast. It was a great way for us to unwind. Their kind words of encouragement convinced us that it was going to be all right. Blessed to have met such warm and friendly people we expressed our sincere gratitude, and appreciation then started out in search of our new home.

We left Lake Charles with renewed faith as our burdens lifted with each mile of the way. Our family was waiting for us in Texas and we were glad things were looking up. We arrived in San Antonio four to five hours later. We were greeted with plenty of hugs, kisses and tears. It had been a while since our last visit. There were many questions in need of answers and many decisions to consider, but right now, it would have to wait until tomorrow.

The next day everyone awakened in good spirits. Well rested we had a chance to revisit in our minds the events of the last three days. Mabel and Jim Medlock are our family. When we were facing the dilemma of whether to evacuate it was the Medlocks who insisted we bring the whole family to San Antonio. The Medlocks are not blood relatives. When my husband was a boy he spent a lot of time in their home, and they made sure he stayed out of trouble. They shared a special closeness, and they loved him as much as he loved and respected them. We always refer to the Medlocks as family, because that's what they are; and will always remain.

In the days that followed we met with Pastor Keith Graham; a true man of God. He and his wife Denetrice have dedicated themselves to doing God's work. Their mission is saving souls and enriching lives through the blessings of Jesus Christ. It would be through Pastor Keith, his wife Denetrice and their congregation that God would continue to bestow his blessings upon us.

Pastor Keith introduced us to the NOW WORD CHRISTIAN CHURCH, and they welcomed us warmly. They were a sincere group of people who made it their mission helping us to get on our feet. They came bearing gifts of every kind, food, clothes, furniture, and bedding. Whatever our needs were they tried to provide. NOW WORD CHRISTIAN CHURCH became our benefactors assisting us financially as well as spiritually. The biggest blessing we received was a spacious house equipped with washer and dryer, televisions sets in every room and a computer. We had everything we needed for a new start, but it was too early to make any permanent decisions. We lived in this nice home for months. Within that time, we spent our days applying for assistance through the Federal Government. Everywhere we went there were long lines; sometimes we spent hours waiting in lines for everything from food stamps to financial assistance. We would leave early in the morning returning in the evening exhausted both physically and mentally.

Each day we relied on the News for updates on conditions back home. There were still a lot of uncertainties, then finally six weeks later the news we had hope for arrived. The suburbs outside of New Orleans where my family lived had begun receiving its citizens, and encouraged everyone who lived there to return home. Everyone was excited about finally going home. I was filled with mixed emotions, happy for them; but sad for me. My home was located within the city limits where conditions had not improved; therefore, it would be a while before my husband, and I could return.

After everyone left, I tried to keep busy finding things to do with my time, but sometimes depression got the best of me. That is why in times like these you have to focus spiritually and mentally relaying on the Holy Spirit for guidance. Therefore, I worshiped with the Now Word Family throughout my stay in San Antonio. This experience increased, renewed and inspired my faith in God.

My husband and I were able to return home six weeks after the others. I believe in my heart that everything we've been through was for a reason and only God knows the reason why.

Today we are back in Louisiana picking up the pieces of our lives. The people we encountered along the way all provided us with hope. Their acts of kindness, words of encouragement, and prayers have meant so much to our recovery. We sincerely appreciate each and every one of them. It's nice to know there are still people out there who care. I wish I could include the names of every person we encountered. There were so many along the way, people like Irene, Kym, Cheryl, Pat, Bonnie, Lolita, Chris, Greg, and the hotel clerk in Lake Charles , but since that is not possible; I will always remember them in my heart.

We are Hurricane Katrina survivors, God delivered us out of the floodwaters of Hurricane Katrina, onto a road of hope where Angels in our midst watched over us. Thank You God for revealing our Angels to us, through them our burdens were lighten!

WANTED

Don't know why it happened
Don't know how
But the destruction that it has caused
Makes me say WOW!

Everywhere I look there's evidence of a crime
So many clues I'm about to loose my mind

There are two main suspects Katrina and Rita
The magnitude of their crime is more than a misdemeanor

They ram sacked houses; turned lives upside down
The destruction can be seen from miles around

Abandon businesses, streets and playgrounds
Everywhere you look it's like a ghost town

If you see these criminals get out of their path
Before you suffer their terrible wrath.

Alex Simmons
Age 10

THE POST KATRINA BLUES

Some days I wake up happy, other days I wake up sad
Some days I'm very thankful, other days I'm extremely mad
One day it's my beginning; the next day it's my end
It's hard to have all the answers when you can't see around the bend
My heart tells me to rebuild, my mind tells me no
My friends tell me to move on, but sometimes I just don't know
Some days I can beat this depression, other days I sadly lose
I know I am only suffering from the post Katrina Blues

Some days it's hard to handle, other days it's a piece of cake
Some days I feel like giving up but a little voice says, "wait"
Some days I move quickly
Other days I move slow
Some days I move in circles
Not knowing which way to go
Everyone has an opinion on what my life should be
It's not plain and simple; it's complicated to me
Some days I can beat this depression, other days I sadly lose
I know I am only suffering from the Post Katrina Blues

My life isn't perfect, that's easy for me to see,
But I don't need pity, or anyone's sympathy
Everyday I try to determine what is best for me
The answer was not in the floodwaters, it's deep within me
Some days I can beat this depression, other days I sadly lose
I know I am only suffering from the Post Katrina Blues

LINES

I arrive early, it's still dark
Hoping to get a safe place to park
Disaster assistance is what I seek
Long lines and no vacant seats.
FEMA, SBA, and RED CROSS; designed to help people
recover from their lost
Lines, lines everywhere I go; waiting in line is the rich, and
the poor
Lines, lines everywhere I go; how long will I wait, I don't
know

Food stamp line to the right; unemployment line to the left
Wait until your name is called before you approach the
desk
It doesn't matter what department; it's always the same
Sign your name, take a number, and don't complain

Don't be in a hurry; sometimes it takes all day
Bring a book to read, to pass the time away
There is no discrimination; everyone is treated the same
Katrina leveled the playing field in this waiting game
Lines, lines everywhere I go; waiting in line is the rich, and
the poor
Lines, lines everywhere I go, how long will I wait, I don't
know

RELAX AND TAKE FIVE

When confusion in your life is at an all time high
And trouble is creeping in on you from all sides
Running out of time; and almost out of hope
So many changes you're at the end of your rope
Free yourself from the madness; it's a state of mind
Pull yourself together, relax and take five

Forms to fill out, but there's too much red tape
Gas prices soaring, you need skates
Bill collectors calling every single day
Trying to collect what Katrina didn't take
Tried to shake it off, but it feels like dead weight
Tried praying about it; but you're running low on faith

Rebuild or demolish; do you have a choice
Is anyone listening, do you have a voice
Insurance companies giving you the blues
Every single day you're feeling abused
Free yourself from the madness; it's a state of mind
Pull yourself together, relax and take five

Your FEMA trailer is short on space
You're homeless, angry and displaced
 Katrina syndrome is too much to take
Will someone please make it go away?
Free yourself from the madness; it's a state of mind
Pull yourself together, relax and take five

LIFE IS A GAMBLE

Everything we do in life is a gamble, sometimes we win, and sometimes we lose.

Therefore, it was the same with Hurricane Katrina. One roll of the dice and we lost it all. Our government officials gambled our levees system would withstand another hurricane season; they lost. Many of our citizens gambled the hurricane would make a turn; they lost. Some citizens took a gamble on riding it out; they lost, but this does not make them losers it makes them determined. We are more determined than ever to fight harder for the things we love about our city and neighborhoods.

We don't know when or where the next major disaster will strike. It could be New Orleans again, or it could be wherever you live. Mother Nature is becoming very unpredictable, and hasn't shone favor on any of us lately.

Today we are all getting ready to roll the dice again with our decision to rebuild or not. Many of you are wondering why, Why would we take such a gamble when we could easily walk away? For some this would be a no brainier, but for those of us who love New Orleans and call it home we are willing to take such a gamble. We love red beans and rice on Mondays and fried seafood on Fridays. We love gumbo, jambalaya, crawfish boils, and cold drinks. In addition, we love traveling short distances, a Sunday afternoon drive along Lake Pontchartrain, and a stroll through the French Quarters, and because we love what many of you can't understand, you win some, you lose some, but you still take a chance!

AFTER THE RAIN

THE SCRAP BOOK

A few years ago, when my oldest son was born, I received a scrapbook as a gift. It was a beautiful book with soft pastel colors of yellow and powdered blue; the edges beautifully trimmed in dove white. On the cover were two large white swans swimming peacefully in a lake as the warm sun shinned on the waters. Its scenic cover gave it a calm and soothing appearance. Inside were plenty of large blank pages to store all my cherished memories of my new son.

I was very excited about my new project, and I immediately began gathering items. This book would be special, and would hold important meaning. It would include photos, announcements, and other special mementos. The first few pages were pictures from the birth to the hospital stay; followed by baby's first few days at home. Then I included photos of grand parents, and great grand parents on both sides of the family. The next few pages were of extended family such as aunts, uncle's cousins, and close friends. I also included baby's first everything. His first fallen tooth, finger painting, report card, certificates, and awards; anything I thought would be sufficient in telling the story of who he was.

The years flew by quickly as I watched my little boy change before my eyes. I adored him and watched with mixed emotions as I loosened the apron strings that held his independence.

Upon approaching my son's tenth birthday, the good Lord blessed us with another addition to the Simmons household. My hands were full once again; and with eagerness, I immediately began entering the new baby's memories into the scrapbook. The book began to fill quickly as I added photos of vacations, and other special events.

As the seasons changed, the boys grew. They began to love the outdoors, and their involvement in outdoor activities kept me very busy. Their participation made my free time in the evenings and weekends almost nonexistent. With so little time available, the scrapbook was set aside.

These days all of my personal projects were on hold including the scrapbook. With the promise of getting back to it, I carefully placed it in a large hard plastic bag, and stored it in a safe place.

Time seemed like it would never slow down and we were spending plenty time away from home. The boys were moving and changing like the metamorphosis of butterflies and I made sure I had plenty of film on hand to capture their transformation. One day I realized things were beginning to pile up; there were pictures in boxes, bags and hampers everywhere but in the scrapbook.

A few years later

We intended to return home within a few days, but to our surprise, it would be months before we could return to our city, but not our home. The hurricanes floodwaters damaged our home. Because it was extensive, we had to find temporary housing. We manage to find a place a few miles near our home; close enough for us to travel back, and forth in order to start the clean-up process. Our home was in ruins; nothing could be salvaged although I tried; but to no avail. The clean up would take weeks even with everyone's help. Each time I returned home, I shed a river of tears.

One day while taking inventory of our damaged property, I remembered the scrapbook. No one had seen it. I could hardly remember the last time I saw it. My life at that time became so busy; I had forgotten where I stored it. At first, I thought it washed away in the flood, but there was no evidence. I immediately began a desperate search to find the missing book.

I searched bedroom closets, boxes stored in closets, the utility room, under beds, on top of shelves; including the attic but my searched turned up nothing. I then became depressed. It was important for me to find the scrapbook, because it was the one thing that linked my children to their past.

Days had gone by, and still no sign of the scrapbook. Where could it be? I was beginning to think I would never find it, and almost gave up hope. Then while clearing out a hall closet that served as the last stop for unwanted and outdated items; I got a surprise. I placed my hand on the top shelf, and felt something very familiar. It was something with a hard plastic covering. I could not believe it; my heart skipped a beat as I immediately realized what it was. There enclosed in the same plastic bag I stored it in years ago was the scrapbook. It was a welcome sight. It had been undisturbed and unharmed by the vicious floodwaters. The hard plastic did a good job of keeping moisture and water from seeping in. No one could imagine the joy I felt at that very moment. Hurricane Katrina left us with the one possession that meant the most to us; the scrapbook.

Today I keep the scrapbook on a table where everyone can see it. We have all added to it and several new books since then. Now that I have recovered it, I can move on with peace of mind. Who would have thought the Simmons boy's heritage would survive the floodwaters of Hurricane Katrina because of a little scrapbook!

A FISH NAMED ROGER

A few years ago, my youngest son Alex wanted a pet. He asked if he could have a dog or cat, but it was out of the question. Our reason for objecting was very simple; Alex was seven and not quite ready for this kind of responsibility. We learned from first hand experience with our oldest son Cedric, having a pet soon becomes the parent's responsibility.

Alex is a humble child, a good student and always does as told. He rarely asks for anything, and when he does, we try to grant his request. A few years went by; before Alex came to us again requesting a pet; this time we gave in. We wanted to give him the perfect pet, one that didn't require a lot of attention from him or us. We considered a cat or a dog only for a brief moment before deciding on a fish. Alex may have been the perfect child in many ways but he never liked cleaning his room. It became a major factor in our decision. Alex was a little disappointed with our decision to give him a fish, but got over it quickly; all the same, he was excited about having a pet.

Alex loved his new friend and every day he was sure to check on him before school, after school and before bedtime. We were all very happy that he was so attentive, but rather surprised that he had not yet named him. We asked Alex about the delay and he replied he was searching for the perfect name. Weeks went by and the fish still didn't have a name. We offered no suggestions, because we wanted it to be Alex's choice.

One day Alex came rushing into the room extremely excited. He had finally found the perfect name for his fish. He proudly informed us he had chosen the name Roger. We tried hard to contain our laughter, and hoped that our facial expressions didn't show. Alex was pleased with the name he had chosen, but we thought it was the funniest name we had ever heard of for a fish.

In the weeks and months that passed, Alex gave Roger a lot of attention; he kept him feed and his bowl clean. Alex thought Roger was the greatest fish in the world and loved showing him off to his friends. Roger demonstrated his love for Alex by swimming rapidly around his bowl the moment he approached. Alex enjoyed many hours of watching Roger swim while Roger appeared happy enjoying his life as a fish.

Months later

The storm proved to be the worst the city had ever seen, and everyday Alex worried about Roger. He longed for the day he would return home to see his friend again. We finally returned months later fearing the obvious. We parked in our driveway for the first time since our evacuation, the house appeared untouched, and for a brief moment, we felt a glimmer of hope, but once inside all hope faded. We were devastated by what we saw. Hurricane Katrina's floodwaters got up to five feet inside our home. The walls were covered from the ceiling to the floors with thick black mold. The furniture was tossed about, still heavily soaked from the floodwaters. The hard wood floors were buckled from the floodwaters sitting for weeks; nothing appeared to be salvageable.

For months, we assumed the worst regarding Roger's survival, but Alex didn't give up hope. The minute the front door opened, Alex rushed to find Roger. Roger did not survive. Roger was found on the floor of the soggy carpet; his bowl was in pieces. It appeared he died sometime ago. Saddened by Roger's death we found a dry place under a fig tree in the back yard, and gave Roger a proper New Orleans burial. Alex was very pleased.

In the weeks that passed, Alex didn't talk about Roger. We knew he missed him terribly. A few weeks later out of concern, we asked Alex if he would like it if we purchased him another fish. Alex's answer surprised us all. He sadly replied, "Roger was a member of our family, and family members could never be replaced." Alex's reply made me realize something very important. Everything we went through regardless of how bad it was we all managed to survive. Every family member had been located and reported to be safe. It would have been very difficult to accept if I had lost even one member of my family. Each person in a family is special, and plays an important role in helping the family to become a complete unit. Alex is right, family members can't be replaced, and I fully understand the reason for his decision. Roger may have been just an ordinary fish to us, but to Alex he was special, and an important member of our family.

THE DAY HURRICANE KATRINIA CHANGED OUR LIVES

Everyone evacuated safely except my niece despite all warnings, she decided to remain behind with her boyfriend and their baby. We tried desperately to persuade the both of them to leave, but they were determined to ride it out. Her boyfriend was convinced the hurricane would make a last minute turn. We pleaded with her to leave for the sake of the baby, but our pleas were unsuccessful. With worry and concern for their safety, we departed.

After the storm all forms of communication was lost. It would be days before we would hear from my niece again. Their decision to stay behind would change their lives forever. Here is their story.

I watched sadly, as my family drove off without me. They begged me to take my baby and leave, but I made a choice to stand by my man no matter what. In the name of love, I remained. Without a second thought, I let my heart overrule my good sense and stayed behind. If I had known how close I would come to facing death, I would not have been so foolish.

The apartment we shared was on the second floor of a sturdy brick building. It was and old building, but still firm and solid. My boyfriend was totally convinced we would be safe if we stayed. He is a very stubborn individual with strong opinions. He felt the media had over played the hurricane's strength and it would make a last minute turn. He was confident in his decision and I trusted him. His logic was because we were located above the first floor; we would be safe from any flooding. We had enough food and supplies needed to ride it out and we were not alone; almost all of the tenets in our building remained.

As the day came to a close Hurricane Katrina reported to become a direct hit. We remained glued to the television the entire night. The night grew long and the city was quite for the first time that I could ever remember. Hurricane Katrina's strength intensified as conditions in the city deteriorated. The winds began to pick up outside, and the rain began to fall as Katrina made her way inland. We kept watch for the arrival of the most dangerous storm in our memory. Hurricane Katrina was expected to make landfall shortly after daybreak on Monday morning.

Night faded as Monday morning slowly crept in. The weather began to change drastically, Outside you could hear the sound of cans and debris being tossed about by forceful winds as Katrina arrived. We dared not look out the window in fear of flying debris. Hurricane Katrina tormented the city with her impact for a few hours before moving on. There were power outages everywhere and it was extremely hot and humid from the heat, but thank God, the daylight made it easy to see. When we felt it was safe we opened the front door for a quick evaluation. It was clear that Katrina had done some damage, but not nearly as what was predicted.

At first, it appeared all predictions were wrong. New Orleans was still standing and had survived a category four hurricane; but this would soon change. One minute we were outside in front the apartment evaluating the damage and all was well. Suddenly we heard a loud noise like a blast preceded by another blast, it sounded as if someone had dropped a bomb. Within minutes, we were standing in a foot of water. Water slowly began creeping up to the second step of the apartment building. It appeared to be coming out of nowhere; people began spilling out into the streets trying to figure out where it was coming from. My first thought was a main water line had busted. We rushed back into the house as the water began to rise. We were unprepared for the horror that followed.

Water was everywhere and rapidly rising. The downstairs apartment began to flood. We didn't know what was happening but, we knew we would drown if we stayed. All electrical power and communications including cells phones were down. Outside in the street we could hear the sounds of people screaming, and yelling; as a state of emergency was developing. In total confusion, we rushed around trying to figure a way out of the apartment. It was unbelievable; water now completely covered the downstairs apartment slowly making its way into ours. Never have I been this scared in my entire life, I tried to stay calm for the sake of my child, but the possibility of us all drowning to death was too much for me to handle. My boyfriend promised me that it wasn't going to end like this, not here, not now and not today. Suddenly I began crying hysterically as I felt my body become too weak to move, but somehow I managed to find the strength to hold on.

My boyfriend was like a mad man in search of some unknown thing. Suddenly a light inside his head must have come on, because what he did next surprised me. I noticed him dragging the king size air mattress we slept on over to the slide glass door that led to the balcony. The next thing I knew he threw it over the side of the railing. Then he grabbed the baby and me, and ushered us out onto the balcony. He had devised a plan to climb down the balcony's railings into the floodwaters. Upon instruction, I was to lower the baby down to him, and then I would proceed to climb down onto the mattress that would serve as a raft. With the baby and me aboard, he would wade along side guiding us to safety. His plan appeared to make sense considering our circumstance, but there was one problem; I couldn't swim and was always afraid of drowning. He convinced me that the only choice I had was floating on the mattress or drowning; in this case, the choice was perfectly clear.

I followed my boyfriend's instructions and did exactly as I was told. We landed safely on the mattress into the floodwaters. I was frightened to death but just as determined to live. One hand clung tightly to my daughter as the other clung to the mattress. My boyfriend guided us through the water constantly reassuring me that we were going to be all right. We were not alone in our fight to survive. Hundreds of our friends and neighbors who had stayed behind joined us. As we floated away from the apartment we begin to see people strained on balconies and rooftops; it appeared no one was safe. It seemed like hours had passed before we heard the sounds of helicopters in the sky above us. A sense of joy filled my body as our chance for survival increased.

The helicopter came in closer and people regained hope. Thank God, the rescue team spotted us first, because I was unsure how much longer I could hold on. I was ever so grateful as we were air lifted and on our way to safety. I gave thanks to God for sparing our lives and for my boyfriend's bravery. From the air, we could see the destruction, houses and businesses were destroyed; and trees were down everywhere .We learned a couple of levees caused the flooding. It seemed the entire city had been affected. I felt blessed to have survived.

Today my family and I have relocated to the city of Houston. We have no visible scars from the day hurricane Katrina blew into our lives, but we will remember it forever. .Hurricane Katrina destroyed our way of life back in New Orleans, but ironically, we were given a new one. My boyfriend and I moved into a much better apartment where we are able to live rent-free for eighteen months. Both of us have found jobs and our daughter is enrolled in a good daycare where she is healthy and happy. The best part of this story is my boyfriend and I was married shortly after arriving in Houston. I haven't completely recovered yet, but I do know the next time there is a hurricane coming my way I'm leaving!

SLEEPING WITH THE ENEMY

Hurricane Katrina brought out the best and the worst in all of us, and uncovered the hidden truth about families. Our Katrina experience led us to dispute the phrase "a family that prays together stays together."

Shortly after arriving in Texas, some wonderful people blessed us with a four-bedroom, two-bath house. The house to us was a mansion compared to having been crammed into a hotel room for two days. We welcomed the space.

It was certain the twelve of us were going to have to live together for a while until conditions back home improved. This seemed like a good idea at first; after all, we were one big happy family: just like the Cosbys, right!

Everything seemed to be working out fine that is until the nightmare on Archers Coach began. Now, I know I shouldn't rehash old memories but; life after Katrina wasn't exactly a bed of roses when we all moved in together.

I hope you're sitting down reading this, because what I am about to share with you may surprise you; and then again it may not.

I love family reunions and holiday gatherings, and I love my family dearly. I know they have a lot of love for me as well. However, to live with them in the same house, for more than a few days again, are reasons to commit suicide. The stress of the entire Hurricane Katrina situation had taken its toll on everyone. The fact that we were already a dysfunctional family didn't help any but, believe me when I say; you never know people until you live with them.

The twelve of us settled in and immediately gave thanks for our blessings both big and small. Our nightmare evacuation was beginning to feel more like a dream.

The first couple of days we felt so blessed we walked around all day with smiles on our faces. There was so much love to go around we could have bottled it and sold it to Wal-

Mart. Then shortly after the first week, our true personalities started to make their presence known. It didn't take us long to transform back into a dysfunctional family. At one point, I compared us to the Disney's Channel "Proud Family" with my husband as Oscar and me as Trudy always in the middle and the crazy family of "Roseanne" It was certainly a "Family Feud" all politeness disappeared, and words like togetherness, teamwork, and respect went right out of the window.

At first, little things became annoying, like loud talking, lights on all night and folks partying while others were trying to sleep, all because a few went to bed with the chickens. It seemed we sometimes disagreed on everything. The disputes were over who would do the cooking, shopping, and what brands of foods to buy; you can't please everybody! Next, it was the invasion of one's privacy, who had privacy?

How could I ever forget the war over the television set, some like to sleep with it on, while others wanted it off, and likewise with the radio. I became so sick of hearing "I don't like this, or I like that" I developed a bad case of "Family in my house blues." Numerous times, I found myself quoting the words of Mr. King (not Martin Luther, the other one Rodney) "Can we all just get along!" We had both adults and children getting on each other's last nerves, which were already beginning to unravel.

I knew the lid on this powder keg was soon going to blow. Then finally, it happened. Fireworks sparked like a July fourth celebration. Someone finally set it off! It was the beginning of cutthroat verbal exchanges, dirty looks, ill feelings, and tension so thick you could cut it with a knife. At this point, my sweet and loving family finally agreed on one thing; it was time to go, but where?

The only time they were teaming up now was to side against one another. Little things turned into big things that soon became issues, and then issues turned into plenty of drama. Everyone had a turn at blowing off steam; including me.

My mother used to say, "Too many women in one house is not a good thing, for more reasons than one" now here we were seven women in all fighting for territory. It was my four sisters, my mother-in-law, sister-in-law and me. Each person had her own way of doing things. There were too many chiefs, and not enough Indians, which led to most of our problems. My husband had a rule: never get in the middle of sisters when they are fighting, but these days he was the referee. He made us call a truce. Then he made us promise to listen, compromise and bite our tongues. We had completely forgotten our mother's great words of wisdom "If you can't say anything nice to each other, keep your mouth shut!" We somehow managed to grin and bare it for six weeks without anyone nursing a hole in their tongue or landing on America's Most Wanted.

The day finally came for some to return home, it was music to my ears. We were together so long, I thought I was going to have to check in to a place with straight jackets and padded walls. Oh how I long for the days of old, when it was my husband, my sons, and I. I hope you don't think I was being a little selfish in my thinking, but I bet you, I wasn't the only one who felt this way about their family during the storm. I know many of you have your own horror stories; would you like to share?!

It is amazing how some people in other cultures can live together in peace and harmony. A terrible disaster forced us together, and we had to pray hard to keep from killing each other. The good thing is we managed to survive the nightmare on Archers Coach, and the entire Hurricane Katrina experience. We also learned a lot about each other and ourselves. I honestly think God gave us exactly what we needed to maintain our own level of sanity. Believe me this experience was a good lesson on relationships.

I thank God for blessing me with a family who can forgive, forget, and laugh about it. To have a family that love and care for each other is a beautiful thing. I would be lost without mine. Guess what! I just remembered something else our mother used to say, "You can choose your friends, but you can't choose your family!" and I 'm glad you can't because, I love them just the way they are. You have your family, and I have mine. One thing you can bet on, with this much love, I won't be sleeping with the enemy again, if I can help it!

MY LIFE 'S PURPOSE

Sometimes when we are faced with obstacles, it is God putting us to a test.

He wants to make sure we will be ready, and able to receive the blessing he has in store for us. I believe a lesson learned is a blessing earned, and some of life most valuable lessons are often learned in the face of danger.

A few years ago prior to writing my first book I was on an emotional roller coaster experiencing twist and turns, and ups and downs. It seemed like no matter how hard I tried I couldn't get off. It left me emotionally drained, and the person whom I always turned to was dying.

My mother was my best friend. All her life she cared for sick people, and children; never taking time for herself. Then when all the children were grown, and it finally looked like she would get her chance; it would be cut short. One day we received terrible news that mother had a fatal illness, and would be in need of an organ transplant in five years. The news devastated us but with hope and faith, we prepared ourselves for this life-changing event. Within a few days of receiving the news, mother's name was quickly added to the organ transplant list and our wait began.

Time went by slowly as we waited patiently everyday for a call from the transplant coordinator, but nothing happened. Mother's condition worsened. Working in the medical field for many years, I had full knowledge of mother's condition, and knew that in her case no news was not good news. I finally consulted her doctors. They gave me the one answer I wasn't looking for. Mother's illness had seriously begun affecting other vital organs. Now the transplant of an organ was no longer an option. This news was like a death sentence. I could not accept nor allow myself to become the bearer of bad news. Therefore, I never told my mother, or anyone else; what I had learned. I couldn't bring myself to take away

Mother's hope, or cause the rest of the family to fall apart. I suffered in silence and lived with the guilt.

Time was of the essence, and with each day that passed mother's condition worsened. I always felt mother suspected there would be no transplant. She never questioned the doctors or me about it, but her cheery behavior proved she was putting up a good front. Mother later died within a year of her predicted death sentence from a massage cerebral hemorrhage Her death left me with an empty void; although I had the support of my family, and five siblings; I felt alone.

I love writing; it makes me feel as if I am freeing my spirit. I especially love writing poetry, because I can reveal the real me. It is my passion, as well as my outlet. It is my escape from reality when I am feeling low. In the past, I have written numerous poems, and short stories. After mother's death, I became very depressed my family and friends were so concerned for my well-being they suggested I take a trip.

The Saints was playing the Falcons in Atlanta and it seemed everyone was going. It is always an exciting game when these two rivals meet, before sell-out crowds they would compete to the end. Hundreds of folks would travel to Atlanta for a non-stop weekend of fun. Sometimes Saints fans would plan their family vacations around this exciting event. There is always plenty of trash talking, and a little harmless betting going on. The party starts on Friday and ends at game time. Win or lose everyone is sure to have a good time. I became convinced to go after taking into consideration the fun I would have with my friends.

It was on November 15, 1996 my birthday the day I was to leave for Atlanta; I would discover my life's purpose.

It started out as a perfect day. My plans were all falling into place. I was excited about my trip, and feeling alive for the first time since Mother's death. All I needed to do was make a quick trip to the bank for extra cash. The weather was beautiful, in fact, it was gorgeous, and I was feeling great. I was so busy concentrating on my trip that I became oblivious to what was going on around me. This was my usual banking place and I was familiar with the area so there was no need to suspect suspicious activity. However, after entering the bank's lobby, I can now add hostage to my list of life experiences.

Out of nowhere, an unmasked gunman dressed in a bright orange and yellow vest, wearing a hard hat, and workers' boots disguised as a street worker appeared. It was apparent I caught him off guard. He had his scarf down around his neck leaving his face exposed. He angrily shouted obscenities and demands at me but the only words I understood were "I'm going to blow your head off."

This person was furious with me. I was not supposed to be able to walk right in while he was guarding the main door ;(but I did). He certainly did not need this. How was this going to look to his partners in crime? I on the other hand was petrified, my heart pound. I stood frozen like a deer surprised by a car's headlights with no place to run. He was so angry with me; he tapped his cold revolver against my forehead to emphasize his point. I somehow managed to move my feet as he lead me to the main lobby.

Inside, I saw other customers lying face down on the floor, laying next to one of them was the bank's nervous unarmed security guard. Across the room at the teller's windows were frightened Tellers trying to carry out the other gunman's demands; every move they made was critical. Their hands were shaking nervously as they carefully tried not to make any mistakes. Judging from everyone's reaction my unexpected presence did not sit too well. I obviously complicated the situation by placing the look out person in an awkward position with his friends.

In what seemed like hours, but instead only minuets my life stood hanging in the balance. I had seen the gunman's face, and could possibly identify him if captured. The question then became what to do with me. It took only a split second for them to decide they didn't need a kidnapping charge added to the list of many if captured.

Next, I heard the sound of police sirens approaching then frantic Robbers scrambled to make their get away. The gunman who held me shoved me to the floor then rushed out of the bank leaving me shaken but unharmed.

Outside the police engaged in gunfire with the robbers. Later I found out one of the Police Officers received several gunshot wounds. The gunmen fled making their way to the Texas state line before their capture.

In the days, and months that followed I wrote continuously. I wrote about my experience as well as my feelings about life and death. One day I happened to share my work for the first time with some friends; it surprisingly sparked some interest. They were constantly urging me to take it to the next level. With the help of friends and much research I self-published my first book. "From the Corners of My Mind" became a hit with the support of family and friends.

One day while shopping in Barnes and Nobles, I met the store manager. After sharing my story with her, she offered to review my book. A few weeks later, she called to give me exciting news. Barnes and Nobles offered me my first professional book signing. The signing was a sweet success it led to more signings, pretty soon I was doing signings at the Essence Festival and in major cities. As the first book gained in popularity there was a request for a second book and "Deep in My Soul" was born. I learned there were people out there who related to some of the same experiences and feelings. Today both books are available in local bookstores as well as in several Barnes and Nobel in Louisiana and Mississippi.

My ordeal was a horrible experience. It challenged my faith in God; as well as renewed it. Through my experiences, I have come to understand, and accept life as a wonderful gift, and no matter how long or how short a time we are given; the only thing that matters is the lives we have touched and made better along the way.

I finally released myself from the guilt of not telling my mother about the transplant; I know in my heart she understood. I was also able to finally come to grips with the lost of my seven year old brother whose life was taken by a driver on the corner of our house when I was sixteen.

I know now the things I have been through; mother's death, my little brother's death, the bank robbery, losing my home, job, and city to Hurricane Katrina has been my true test of faith. All of these events have led me to my life's purpose,

My writings helped me to find my way through the darkness into the light. I know now my life's purpose is to share my true-life experiences with others to help encourage and inspire them. To help others recognize and acknowledge God's presence in every aspect of our lives, in good times and in bad times. I would have never imagined out of the floodwaters of Katrina, I would discover my life's Purpose!

CHANGES

Life is about changes, and everything in life must change in order for there to be Progress. Sometimes the change is so gradual you hardly even notice. Then sometimes change happen so rapidly you can hardly keep up. Fast or slow change must take place.

Life takes us through a serious of changes everyday. Times change, people change, things change, even we change, because it is necessary for our growth and survival. We can embrace it or we can go through it kicking and screaming, standing still or moving forward changes will occur.

Six months ago my life experienced sudden change, and everything about my life as I knew it changed with it. Hurricane Katrina blew into my life and took everything except my memories. The house, job, family, friends, and city leaving no stone unturned.

Each morning I awake in a world that is not mine. For me the city I temporarily reside in is a foreign land. The house is not mine, the furniture all donated, the bed I sleep in is not mine and the people in the neighborhood are all strangers. I find myself in a world of changes, which occasionally leaves me with bouts of depression. Sometimes it's a day-to-day struggle just to get up in the morning. Sometimes I shed tears and long for my old life to return. Then suddenly I regain the strength to see beyond myself, pass the strangers, and pass the material things I once cherished and everything that is different, and I become spiritually inspired. I know I am not alone, there are thousands of stories of men and women just like me who have experienced similar changes, and are fighting to rebuild their lives as well.

Today, right here and now, I am fighting for my life. What I have been through is just a temporary set back. The reason I am sharing my story is maybe through my life someone else can find the hope, and strength that I have found. I realize I can drown in my tears and let the old me continue to drown in the floodwaters of Katrina, or I can change my attitude and help the new me fight even harder to survive.

Always remember life is about change, if we change our attitudes, we can change the game. Right now, I am smiling on the inside even if you can't see my face, because I know Katrina may have won the rally, but I'm winning the game!

BRIDGE OVER
TROUBLED WATERS

TROUBLED WATERS

Troubled waters, Troubled times
Troubled people, Troubled minds

Rushing water, levees breached
Water spilling into the streets
Finger pointing who's the blame?
Louisiana politics hasn't changed

Missing children, families displaced
Each new day is a test of faith
Water above ceilings, people trapped on roofs
No one coming to their rescue

Troubled water, Troubled times
Troubled people, Troubled minds

Folks wade in water above the waist
While some float on mattresses and crates
Where are the buses, planes, and vans?
The government says their doing all they can
Washed up cities, washed up homes
Historic buildings all gone

People need answers; will someone explain
How cans this happen in God's name?
These are Americans; not refugees
Will someone please attend to their needs?

Troubled waters, Troubled times
Troubled people, Troubled minds

I BELONG TO GOD

Whenever I'm feeling lonely
And there's no one
To share my thoughts
And problems troubling me
Are weighing on my heart

I look around the world
And behold God's wondrous love
And say to myself
"I belong to God"

For each day I'm awakened
By the power of God's command
And every mountain I face today
Is in God's trusting hands

I'm inspired by his love
To forgive my fellow man
And in spite of his unkindness
He is only just man

When people define who I am
By the color of my skin
And miss out on a chance
To have me as a friend

Suddenly I'm reminded
Of God's wondrous love
And say to myself
"I Belong to God'

MY LIGHT

Open up the window
Let me see God's face
As he elevates my spirit
To a holy place

Let the angels bring
The good news
That causes my soul to shout
And all men believe
Without a shadow of a doubt

Open up the window
So others can see my light
Someone may need
Safe harbor tonight

Let me stand like a lighthouse
On a friendly shore
Where my light can be
Seen all over the world

My light is there to guide
All men safely in
To a place where God is love
And to every man a friend

Let my light shine in places
Where reckless souls are lost
Let my light lead them
Safely out of the dark

(Cont.)

Open up the window
Let me see God's face
As he elevates my spirit
To a holy place

LOST AND FOUND

Lost in the world
A long way from home
I foolishly embraced
The things I knew were wrong

The road I traveled
A tortuous plain
I experienced heartache and
A lot of pain

When friends tried to help
I refused their advice
Sinking deeper into misery
Taking a gamble on my life

With my back against the wall
And my head hanging low
I remembered what I was taught
A long time ago

God answers prayers if you go
To him for help
Put away your foolish pride
And give of yourself

Forgiveness is a gift
God unselfishly extends
It doesn't matter what you've done
He'll wipe away your sins

If you are lost in the world
And can't find your way
Put aside your foolish pride
And get on your knees and pray

ARE YOU READY?

The Day of Judgment
Is coming soon
Will you declare a victory?
Or eternal doom

Will you answer his call
When you hear his voice?
Will you be steadfast and true
And make him your choice?

When he calls you
Out of the darkness
Into his marvelous light
Will you put on the whole armor
And be prepared to fight?

When your burdens get heavy
Will you pick up the pace
And be bound and determined
To finish the race?

Will you honor him before men
And as your savior and friend
Or will you deny the truth
And die in your sins?

Will you love him unconditionally?
As he loves you
You have a decision to make
Which will you choose?

UNLOCK THE TREASURE

If you're looking for the gift
That no man can measure
Look no further unlock the treasure

An eternity of happiness is at your feet
Heavenly treasures and Jesus is the key
Jesus is the key to a land of milk and honey
Healing streams, green pastures and
Everyday is sunny

No sickness, or sorrow, worries or cares
The angels and saints are all gathered there
Everyday will be Sabbath, people never grow old
The streets are paved with silver and gold

If you're looking for the gift
That no man can measure
Look no further unlock the treasure

You're one step away from finding the key
If you're pure in heart and its Jesus you seek
Jesus can wash you whiter than snow
From the Lamb of God all blessings flow

God's Kingdom awaits you and me
All the treasures of heaven and Jesus is the key
So much is in store for an unworthy soul
Blessing from heaven silver and gold

If you're looking for the gift
That no man can measure
Look no further unlock the treasure

SUKETHER'S LAGNIAPPE

FAMILY

The other day I was thinking how long it has been
The last time we gathered family and good friends.
As I reminisce, the picture becomes clear
Like the scene at grandma's house a festive holiday one
    year.
Those good ole family gatherings I remember them well
Family, food, fun, and exaggerated tales

It would all start in the kitchen of grandma's wood frame
    house
Folding chairs and card tables were sure to be put out
On the dinning room table lay a magnificent feast
Turkeys, hams, fixings and other delicious treats

We would gather around the table with everyone joining
    hands
It was always important to thank the man upstairs
The blessing was always lead by the eldest of the group
There was sure to be lots of amen's before the prayer was
    through

Once seated at the table we enjoyed a feast for a king
As conversations of various subjects would quickly begin
Heads turn in every direction as laughter filled the air
Everyone carried on without a worry or care

When everyone was caught up on all the latest news
They eased away from the table if they could move
One by one, they strolled into the family room
In search of a comfortable place to digest their food
The men would call a meeting to discuss family matters
Some place nice and quite away from all the chatter

(Cont.)

Meanwhile in the living room the party is about to start
Some one is playing the latest songs from the music charts
Bodies moving and shaking, folks dancing everywhere
They quickly make a dance floor by removing all the chairs

The sound of music awakens Uncle Willie from his nap
He funky chicken to the dance floor while Aunt Dorothy
    finger snaps
The electric slide is done by the entire group
But it's the second line that signifies the end of the day is
    through
Good ole family gatherings, I remember them well
Lots of food, fun and exaggerated tales

IF I COULD HAVE MY WAY

You asked me what I wanted
If I could have my way
I'd like to grow wings
And one day fly away
High into the heavens
Where the sky is blue
And clouds form the moisture
That makes the morning dew

I would travel to the place
Between time and space
In search of the secret
That would shield our minds from hate
I would secure it under my hat
And safely bring it back
You asked me what I wanted
Is this to much to ask?

If I could have my way
I would make rainbow colored people
With shades including lime
And every dark cloud
Will have a silver line
Good guys will always win
And bad guys will always lose
And no one will ever wake –up
With Monday morning blues
\

(Cont.)

I would like to have the dream
That Dr. King spoke of
Where children play together
In the name of love
Where the sun shines on my face
And the wind is at my back
You asked me what I wanted
Is this to much to ask?

You asked me what I wanted
If I could have my way
I would like to grow wings
And one day fly away!

DOWN HOME NEW ORLEENS

Give me a seafood platter, gumbo, and some spicy red
     beans
There's nothing like the taste of
Down home New Orleens

Praline candy and beignets are a few of our tasty treats
Boiled crawfish is one dish you need instructions on how
     to eat
There's nothing like the sound of jazz when it's heard on
     Bourbon Street
You haven't seen a dog gone thing until a second line comes
     down the street

Exotic dancers and street musicians will always put on a
     show
If you want a real good time New Orleans is the place to go
Mardi Gras is the perfect day to be who you want to be
Zulu, and Endymion parades; are a must for you to see

Sip on a drink named Hurricane
Or a root beer named Barqs
Ride the streetcar to the River Walk
Or enjoy jazzing in the park
   If you haven't been to New Orleans, you better make it
   soon
Get plenty of rest; bring your appetite, and your dancing
   shoes

Give me a seafood platter, gumbo,
And some spicy red beans
There's nothing like the taste of
Down Home New Orleens

ENVIRONMENTAL CHANGES

Global warming, hurricanes,
Tornadoes, earthquakes, and acid rain
Seasons changing every week; ozone layer getting weak

Fish swimming in polluted lakes;
contaminated by toxic waste
Forest fires destroying the land, started by careless hands

Environmental changes affects everyone
We're all responsible for what may come
Global warming, hurricanes; let's start
caring, and stop placing blame

Haze in the sky can't breathe the air;
landfills expansions everywhere
Crowded cities, trash filled streets;
dangerous havoc we all reek

Time is running out we're up against the clock
We're dragging our feet it's time we stop
If we bury solutions in red tape; what
will become of the human race?

Let's get back to where the air is clean
Where grass smells new, and the color is green
Where fish swim freely in lakes, and streams
And our future is a reality not a dream
Where snow capped mountains are a beautiful sight
And the stars shine brightly in the night

(Cont.)

Environmental changes affects everyone
We're all responsible for what may come
Global warming, hurricanes; let's start
caring, and stop placing blame

SIXTY YEARS OF LOVING YOU

It's our anniversary
Another milestone for you and me
Celebrating another year
Of life long memories

Sixty Years ago
We exchanged wedding vows
Two people in love
With our heads
In the clouds

Overcoming life's challenges
Together as a team
Working toward a single goal
Of fulfilling all our dreams

Sixty years of watching
A golden sunrise
I could achieve anything
With you by my side

There is no magic potion
For love eternally
Understanding and communication
Is the only key

Each time I reflect
On the things we've been through
I think of that special day
When we said "I do"

(Cont.)

Sixty years have flown,
And physical evidence may show
I still see the person
I fell in love with
Sixty years ago

THE LONELY GAME

Chill the wine, dim the lights
No commitments for tonight
Soft music, a love song
Lose yourself in stranger's arms
It's not meant to be perfect
So don't reminisce
Don't be fooled by
A passionate kiss

Who needs love, that's what they say
It does no good anyway
You give your heart, and then you're burned
View it as a lesson learned
Take your heart and walk away
That's the game the lonely play

Getting close is not for them
They don't want a lover
Just a friend
Play it safe that's the key
Why make it harder than it has to be

In this game there is only one rule
Give into love you'll surely lose
Chill the wine, dim the lights
Someone lonely plays tonight

LIFE RULES FOR TEENS

No drinking until you're twenty-one
No staying out all night
Alcohol, drugs, and cigarettes will
eventually ruin your life.

Be careful who you choose as friends
and who you hang around
And when you're riding in the car; keep the music down
Too much T.V is not good for you
Loud music will make you crazy
Lying around your room all day, will only make you lazy

Don't be fooled by trying to assume; play it safe and ask
And when you're asked to do a job; do it right don't slack
All decisions concerning your life is always in God's hands
And you can achieve anything with hard work and a plan
The road to success is paved with the
things we learn at home
Sometimes we don't appreciate them
until we're on our own

WHERE DID THE TIME GO?

Graduation day is almost here
So many plans for the coming year
Seems like yesterday you started to walk
With help from phonics, you learned to talk

I remember your first day of school
Anxious and excited as I tied your shoes
You held my hand tightly afraid to let go
I cried on the inside so my tears wouldn't show

The years came and went as I watched you grow
We made castles in the sand, and angels in the snow
However, there is one question I'd like to know
Where in the world did the time go?

It seems only yesterday day you attend your first dance
Then suddenly you were twelve, and thinking of romance
It was always my pleasure tucking you in at night
Now I take second place to your social life
Instead of character pajamas, it's a cap and gown
You'll walk across a stage, and stand proud

As I sit and think of the past
There is only one question I continue to ask
Although the answer I already know
Can anyone tell me
WHERE DID THE TIME GO?

ABOUT THE AUTHOR

Sukether Williams Simmons, the author who possesses the ability to speak directly from the heart is attracting readers with her books and down home southern personality. "Mrs. Simmons has found that unique and rare ability to tap into the inner feelings of those who read her work," says New Orleans Tribune Magazine July/August 2003. The first thing you will notice about this Southern girl is her down to earth personality. "She is extremely personable, customers enjoy her enthusiasm, and there is only one word to describe Mrs. Simmons work that word is "AWESOME," says Lindi Weatherford, Community Relations Manager BARNES & NOBLE BOOK SELLERS Metairie, Louisiana.

She is a resident of New Orleans and a native of Jefferson Parish Louisiana. Simmons was educated in both Parishes. She attended the University of New Orleans, and Louisiana Technical College before marring her husband and friend Cedric Simmons Sr. She is the proud mother of Cedric Jr., and Alex (A.J.) who are her life's inspiration.

She is the Author of "From the Corners of My Mind", "Deep in My soul" and her latest work "Down, But Not Out! Reflections of a Hurricane Katrina survivor" books of poetry and short stories that "warms the heart and touches the soul," says reader Pamela Metcalf. "Her books are an inspiration for all ages, books that help you get through the tough times," says another reader Thelma Matthews.

Simmons draws her inspiration for her books from family and personal experiences, she says "everywhere you look there is a story waiting to be told all it needs is the right person to bring it to life! Although Hurricane Katrina devastated her life as well as her home, she is encouraged to rebuild in New Orleans, the city she loves and calls home.

Sukether Simmons temporarily resides in Kenner, Louisiana with her husband and two sons.

Printed in the United States
115102LV00001B/208-228/A

9 781425 942847